FROM ZERO
TO INFINITY

Written by Dr Mike Goldsmith
Illustrated by Andrew Pinder

Edited by Sue McMillan and Elizabeth Scoggins
Designed by Barbara Ward
Cover Illustrated by Hui Skipp
Cover Designed by Angie Allison
and Derrian Bradder

FROM ZERO
TO INFINITY

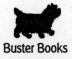

Buster Books

This paperback edition first published in 2017

First published in Great Britain in 2012 by Buster Books,
an imprint of Michael O'Mara Books Limited,
9 Lion Yard, Tremadoc Road, London SW4 7NQ

 www.busterbooks.co.uk f Buster Children's Books 🐦 @BusterBooks

A CIP catalogue record for this book is available from the British Library.

ISBN: 978-1-78055-464-8

1 3 5 7 9 10 8 6 4 2

Printed and bound in February 2017 by CPI Group (UK) Ltd,
108 Beddington Lane, Croydon, CR0 4YY, United Kingdom.

Papers used by Michael O'Mara Books are natural, recyclable products
made from wood grown in sustainable forests. The manufacturing processes
conform to the environmental regulations of the country of origin.

CONTENTS

GET INTO NUMBERS

Do fractions frustrate you? Do numbers drive you nuts? Never fear, this book will take you on a whirlwind tour through the fascinating world of maths, until you're potty for percentages and think decimals are divine!

It's not just about the mechanics of maths though. There are sections in this book about how maths affects all kinds of things, from the way animals behave, to the way you hear music. Lots of the greatest thinkers throughout history loved maths, and used it to invent cool stuff, and discover new things.

Whether it helps you tackle your homework, or teaches you some new facts to freak out your friends, this book will make you a maths-lover, too – guaranteed.

NIFTY NUMBERS

ANCIENT NUMBERS

Long before calculators and computers were invented, if humans wanted to keep a record of things they had counted, they cut lines into sticks or bones. One of the earliest known examples of this kind of counting was discovered in a cave in South Africa. It was a baboon bone with 29 lines scratched into it. Tests show that the scratches were made about 35,000 years ago.

Tally-Ho!

These lines, or tallies, may have been used to count anything from animals or people to passing days.

WATCH OUT – HE'S RUNNING OUT OF BONES!

At first, the only number symbol used was 'I'. Really these were just scratches on bones though, so, if humans wanted to count to 1,000, they had to find a load of baboon bones and scratch 1,000 Is.

Today, there are 10 different digits, or numerals – 0, 1, 2, 3, 4, 5, 6, 7, 8 and 9. These digits make up what is called the decimal system – from the Latin word for ten: *decimus*.

The decimal system is a very logical way for humans to count – most people first learn about numbers when they start to count on their ten fingers. In fact, the word 'digit' also means 'finger'. It's probably how you learned to count and it's probably just how ancient humans started, too.

Count Like an Egyptian

The earliest known counting system based on the number 10 was used 5,000 years ago, in Egypt. The Egyptians used sets of lines for numbers up to nine. They looked something like this:

Their new symbol for 10 was ∩, and larger numbers used combinations of Ⅰs and ∩s. So 22 was written: ∩∩ⅠⅠ. For 100 they used ℚ and for 1,000 𝄃, up to a million: 𝄃.

A million seemed so massive to the ancient Egyptians that it also meant 'any enormous number'.

Timeless Numerals

The Romans also counted in tens, using letters for numbers: I (1), V (5), X (10), L (50) and C (100). Later, D (500) and M (1,000) were added.

To write a number, letters were grouped together, and added up, or taken away, according to the order. For example, if I is placed in front of a letter representing a larger number, it means 'one less than'. IX is nine, or one less than ten. The symbols CL were used to write 150 – or 100 plus 50. So added together the letters CCLVII stand for 257.

You can see Roman numerals on some clocks or at the end of some TV programmes, to show when they were made.

ALL ABOUT NOTHING

People had been using counting systems for centuries before they realized that something was missing – zero! Although an ancient Greek man named Ptolemy did experiment with it, zero wasn't used regularly until the late 9th century.

MOVE ALONG – THERE'S 'NOTHING' TO SEE HERE.

Count Me In

Without zero, there is no way of telling the difference between, say, 166, 1,066 and 166,000. It is also a handy starting point for everything from stopwatches to rulers and temperature scales, too.

To tell the difference, a new counting system of 'positional notation' was developed, using the 'place value' of numbers. This system divides numbers into columns, starting with ones, or units, on the right, with tens to the left, then 100s, then 1,000s, and so on. For example, with the number 3,975, you can easily see that there are three 1,000s, nine 100s, seven 10s and five 1s.

In this system, after you reach 9, you place a 1 in the tens column and go back to 0 in the units column. After 19, the 1 in the tens column changes to a 2 and the units go back to zero again, and so on, until you reach 99. Then a 1 is placed in the 100s column, and the units and tens go back to zero.

11

HOW TO TALK TO COMPUTERS

The ten-digit number system is called 'base 10'. However, there are other bases, too. The most simple is base 2, or 'binary'. It uses just two digits – 1 and 0.

In binary, instead of writing '0, 1, 2, 3, 4, 5, 6, 7' and so on as normal, you would write, '0, 1, 10, 11, 100, 101, 110, 111' to represent the same numbers. This is because, just as in base 10, binary numbers can be thought of in columns. Instead of going up in 1s, 10s, 100s, 1,000s working from the right – increasing by a multiple of 10 each time – the value of the columns doubles each time. From the right, the first column is 1s, the next column to the left is 2s, the next is 4s, then 8s, then 16s, and so on. For example, the number 17 is written as 10001, which means: 'one 16, zero 8s, zero 4s, zero 2s and one 1':

16s	8s	4s	2s	1s
1	0	0	0	1

This might not seem a particularly useful way to count, but it is perfect for computing. Every computer is full of tiny electronic switches, each of which can either be on or off.

242?

NOW SAY IT IN BINARY.

To a computer, a switch that is on represents a 1 and a switch that is off represents 0.

A set of switches in a computer can store a binary number. The number 5, for instance, would be stored like this – well, it would if the computer had elves inside it:

Computers use binary to store and work with all kinds of data, not just numbers. Everything from letters and sounds to pictures, as well as numbers, can be converted into binary code.

Did You Know?

There are many other bases as well as base 10 and base 2. Base 8, or 'octal', and base 64, are also used in computing, as is base 16, or 'hexadecimal', which is used to refer to areas within computer memories. It uses the digits 0, 1, 2, 3, 4, 5, 6, 7, 8, 9 and the letters A, B, C, D, E, and F.

TRICKY OPERATIONS

When you are counting or adding or subtracting, you are performing an 'operation'. Not the kind that doctors perform – the kind that mathematicians perform when they do 'arithmetic'.

The word arithmetic comes from ancient Greek and means 'the art of number'. It includes addition, subtraction, multiplication and division, which are known as the 'four operations'.

Line 'Em Up!

A number line is a good way to think about numbers and operations. Here is a number line showing the addition 2 + 2. The answer, known as the sum, in addition, is of course 4:

Subtraction is just as simple. To calculate 10 – 4, count backwards along the number line from the first number, 10, using the second number, 4.

The answer is the difference between the two numbers. Here, it is 6:

Multiplication is repeated addition. For example, to calculate 3 × 4 using a number line, simply count along from 0 by the first 'factor', or number, as many times as the second factor to get the answer. In multiplication this is known as the 'product'. Here, the product is 12.

Division is repeated subtraction. The example below shows 6 ÷ 3. The number line is marked off from zero to the 'dividend' – the first number – then split into equal segments that match the second number – the 'divisor'. The length of each segment is the 'quotient', which is what the answer is known as in division. Here, it is 2:

For addition and multiplication, it does not matter which way round the calculation is written. 2 + 3 is the same as 3 + 2. However, it's worth remembering that the same is not true for division and subtraction. 7 – 2 is not the same as 2 – 7 and 12 ÷ 3 is not the same as 3 ÷ 12.

NUMBER NAMES

You'll already have noticed that numbers are given a lot of impressive-sounding names. Amaze your maths teacher by knowing your 'integers' from your 'irrationals'. Read on to find out more.

What Do You Mean, Integer?

So far, this book has looked at whole numbers – starting at 0 and running along a number line with 1, 2, 3 and so on. Whole numbers, including 'negative' numbers – those to the left of zero on a number line – are known as 'integers'. Numbers to the right of zero on the number line are known as 'positive numbers'.

Number Shapes

You've probably already heard of 'square' numbers. These are any numbers that can be made by multiplying an integer by itself, such as 4, which is 2 x 2, or 9, which is 3 x 3. Did you know that there are also 'triangular' numbers, though? These are numbers in the series 1, 3, 6, 10 and so on (see page 20).

Irrational Numbers

Numbers are 'rational' if they can be obtained by dividing one integer by another, so ½, 8, 4 ⅔ can be written as 1 ÷ 2, 64 ÷ 8, 14 ÷ 3 respectively, so they are all rational. 'Irrational' numbers, such as the square root of 2* (see page 22), shown as √2, and √47, cannot be written like this.

* A square root is a number that, multiplied by itself, gives a particular number. For example, 4 is the square root of 16 because 4 x 4 = 16.

UNBREAKABLE NUMBERS

Most numbers can be broken down into other smaller whole numbers, or 'factors' (see page 15). For example, 4 can be broken down into two lots of 2.

However, some numbers cannot be broken down in this way, and can only be divided exactly by themselves or by 1. For example, there are no two numbers that 13 can be divided by, except for 1 and 13. Unbreakable numbers like these are called 'prime numbers'. The first few are 2, 3, 5, 7, 11 and 13, but there are other much higher prime numbers that, surprisingly, can still only be divided by themselves or by 1.

Did You Know?

Mathematicians love prime numbers and, although they are easy to understand, they are very mysterious. This is because they don't fit into a regular pattern, so there is no way to find them except by trial and error.

Some mathematicians compete to see who can find the next highest prime number. The most recent one to be found has more than 22 million digits. It's so long that it would take more than four months to write out by hand!

NUMBERS IN NATURE

One way of describing numbers is by saying they are 'odd': 1, 3, 5 and so on – or 'even': 2, 4, 6 and so on. Two odd numbers or two even numbers have what is called the same 'parity' – if you have one odd and one even number, they have different parity. One of the strange things about parity is that it's not a human invention – it turns up in nature, too.

Oddly Even

The majority of animals have an even number of limbs. Humans are 'bipeds', which means they have 2 legs. Horses and dogs are 'quadrupeds', which means they have 4 legs, whereas insects have 6 legs and spiders have 8.

A millipede, meaning 'thousand-legged' in Greek, only has around 300 legs in reality, but it is still an even number.

Nature is so organized that even DNA – the blueprint for how an animal develops – is usually arranged in pairs of an even number of chromosomes. Humans generally have 46 chromosomes arranged in 23 pairs.

How Odd!

In the world of fruit and vegetables, different rules apply, and many of the numbers that relate to plants are odd ones. For example, lots of flowers have five petals, and fruit, such as apples, are based on a five-pointed shape, as you can see if you cut one in half to separate the top and bottom.

Not all the numbers to do with plants have the same parity, but they do have something in common. Pineapples and pine cones have spikes arranged in two sets of spirals, one going clockwise and one anti-clockwise.

Depending on how big the pineapple is, there will be either five and eight spirals, eight and 13 spirals, or 13 and 21 spirals. These are known as 'Fibonacci numbers' (see page 30 for more on these).

Numbers also count in the world of crystals, too. All sorts of things – from salt to snowflakes – are made up of crystals with regular shapes that have a fixed number of sides.

A DEADLY NUMBER

Pythagoras was a Greek mathematician who was born around 580 BCE. He hated beans and loved triangles, and is considered by many to be one of the most important mathematicians ever. Little else is known about him, except that a theorem is named after him, even though he didn't actually come up with the idea for it himself.

Lovely Triangles

Much of Pythagoras's work revolved around triangles. He was fascinated by triangular numbers, such as 3, 6 and 10, which can be arranged in a triangular pattern, like this:

Pythagoras's Theorem

Pythagoras is best known in relation to a theorem about triangles. It is a theorem that only applies to right-angled triangles, which have one horizontal line and one vertical line. The theorem says that if you square the lengths of the two short sides and add them together, the result is the square of the length of the longest side – the 'hypotenuse'.

Here, the sides of the triangle are 3, 4 and 5cm long. The squares of the shorter sides are 9, which is 3 × 3, and 16, which is 4 × 4. If you add 9 and 16 together you get 25, which is 5 × 5, so the hypotenuse is 5cm long.

This is very convenient, as it gives you a way to work out the length of one side of a right-angled triangle, as long as you know the lengths of the other two sides. There's even a handy formula to show your workings out: $a^2 + b^2 = c^2$.

No Beans, Please!

Although the theorem has his name on it, it is thought that Pythagoras actually heard about it in Egypt. The Egyptians and the Babylonians had been using the principle for centuries. However, he did produce some amazing theories himself. These include the basics of the science of sound, the idea that the Earth spins and that 'everything is number'.

Pythagoras and his followers were so secretive that many of their practices and ideas are not known about. Historians do know that as well as not eating beans, Pythagoreans would not sit on pots of a certain size, and didn't allow swallows to nest under their roofs. Unfortunately, no one knows the reason why.

The Terrible Twos

Pythagoras and his followers were known to love simple things that fitted with rules. They were also convinced that all numbers could be expressed as simple ratios – for instance, one quarter is the ratio of 1 to 4, which is written as ¼. Then something was discovered that upset this.

Take a look at this triangle:

It looks perfectly innocent, doesn't it?

However, if you use the formula from the theorem to work out the length of the hypotenuse, things go a bit wrong.

This is because 1 x 1 is just 1. Add the two sides together to get the square of the hypotenuse and you get 2. There's no simple way of showing the number that, when multiplied by itself, gives the answer 2. This number, known as the 'square root', or √2, cannot be written as a ratio – it is an endless number that begins 1.4142 and goes on for ever.

BUT, I ONLY SAID 1.41421356...

This really irritated Pythagoreans, who tried to keep these endless, or irrational numbers, a secret. When one of their followers, Hippasus, kept talking about them, he was thrown to his death from a cliff!

Superstitious Stuff

The Pythagoreans aren't the only ones who dislike certain numbers. Over the centuries, particular numbers have taken on different significance around the world. For example, in China, the number eight is considered very lucky. In other countries, it's the number seven. Some people believe the number 13 to be very unlucky. In fact, there's even a name for the fear of the number 13: triskaidekaphobia.

MICE ARE OKAY, BUT NOT WHEN THERE ARE 13 OF THEM!

How Puzzling

Number puzzles known as magic squares are thought to have originated in China. Over the centuries, some people believed that they could be used to make predictions, which isn't very likely, but they do make a good puzzle!

In a magic square, each row, column and diagonal adds up to a 'constant', which means the 'same number'.

In this one, every row and column and diagonal adds up to 15:

4	9	2	15
3	5	7	15
8	1	6	15
15	15	15	15

15

FAIR SHARES

Imagine it's your birthday and you've got seven friends over for tea. How do you cut your cake into eight equal portions, to make sure that everyone gets a fair share? It's easier than it seems, if you know how ...

Nice Slices

In maths, shares are called 'fractions', so to share your birthday cake fairly between eight people, it needs to be cut into eight equal slices. Another way of saying this would be that each slice is one eighth of the cake. As a fraction, it would be written like this: $\frac{1}{8}$. The top number is called the 'numerator', the bottom number is called the 'denominator'.

Cutting The Cake

Here's how to make fractions work with your cake:

1. First, cut the cake in half ($\frac{1}{2}$), to get two equal pieces.

2. Cut each half in half again, so you have four equal pieces, each of which is now $\frac{1}{4}$ of the cake.

3. Finally, cut each quarter in half again, so that you have eight pieces. Each piece is now $\frac{1}{8}$ of the cake – enough for you and your seven friends to tuck in without arguments.

You may have noticed something else, too. Did you see how the fractions work together? If you halve a half you get a quarter: $\frac{1}{2} \times \frac{1}{2} = \frac{1}{4}$, and if you halve a quarter you get an eighth: $\frac{1}{2} \times \frac{1}{4} = \frac{1}{8}$.

Top-Heavy Fractions

For most fractions, the numerator is smaller than the denominator. These are known as 'proper fractions'.

Occasionally, you might see a more unusual fraction like this: $\frac{11}{2}$. This is an 'improper fraction' because the numerator is bigger than the denominator. The fraction $\frac{11}{2}$ is another way of saying there are '11 halves'.

Imagine these are halves of cake – if they were paired up to make whole cakes, you would have five-and-a-half cakes, or $5\frac{1}{2}$. This is what is known as a 'mixed number', as it's a whole number followed by a fraction.

Perfect Percentages

What if you could divide your cake into 100 slices instead of just eight? If you wanted a quarter of the cake, you would have to take 25 slices, or $^{25}/_{100}$. This can also be written as 25 'per cent' or %, which means '25 out of 100' – really 25% is just another way of saying ¼.

Demystifying Decimals

Another way to think of fractions is as a division calculation. If you use the cake example, ¼ tells you to 'divide 1 cake into 4 pieces'. If you tapped 1 ÷ 4 into a calculator, the answer would be: 0.25. This is what is known as a 'decimal fraction' – sometimes they are called 'decimals' for short.

If you put 1 ÷ 3 into a calculator, the answer will be 0.3333333 ..., which goes on for ever. This is called a 'recurring fraction'. To save space, they are written with a dot over the recurring part, so $^{1}/_{3}$ is written as $0.\dot{3}$.

How About Rounding?

Sometimes, a number will have lots of digits after the point. For example, the number 0.4567 has four. This is called working to four decimal places. These numbers can be shortened by 'rounding' up or down. If you wanted to work to two decimal places instead, you would look at the digit in the third decimal place – if it is greater than 5, as with 0.4567, you would round up to 0.46. If it is less than 5, as with the number 0.6543, you would round the number down to 0.65.

MONEY, MONEY, MONEY

In ancient times, people didn't use money; they swapped or bartered things, such as cattle. Let's face it though, cattle aren't that easy to transport, so an alternative was needed.

> SORRY SIR, YOUR CATTLE HAVE BEEN DECLINED.

In the early days of money, people used natural objects that were fairly rare and small enough to be carried easily – these could be anything from the shells of cowrie sea snails to feathers. Metal coins started to be used around 700 BCE in Lydia, which is now part of Turkey, and in China. Even so, if people were travelling long distances, or buying and selling huge sums, they still had to carry large, heavy bags of coins. In 12th century China, this problem was solved by the invention of paper money.

Invisible Money

That's not the end of the story though. Nowadays, most of the world's money is stored on computer and is transferred electronically between banks, shops and people.

How Interesting

You might already have your own bank account, and maybe your savings are already earning 'interest', but how do you tell your interest from inflation, and what are they?

The idea of interest is quite simple. You put some money in a bank account and the bank uses it to earn money for itself. In return, you get some extra money, called 'interest'. If you borrow money from a bank, you are charged interest on it, meaning you have to pay back more than you borrow.

The amount of interest you earn or pay depends on three things – the amount of money paid into or borrowed from the bank, the 'rate' of interest the bank offers, and the length of time the money is in the account or borrowed for. Say the bank offers a rate of 10 % interest a year on savings, and £200 is paid in and left there for a year. After that year, it will have made 10 % of £200, which is £20. This means that at the end of the year, there will be £220.

Up and Up

Almost everything gets more expensive over time. Like interest, 'inflation' is described by a percentage. If inflation is 5% one year, and a chocolate bar costs £1, it is likely to cost £1.05 in a year's time.

Ideally, most people's wages go up at about the same rate as inflation, so they can keep pace with price increases.

ONE AFTER ANOTHER

In maths, an ordered row of numbers is called a sequence. Sequences usually have a pattern, or a rule, that allows you to predict the next number. Counting puts numbers into about the simplest sequence there is. In the sequence below, 1 is added to the previous number:

$$1, 2, 3, 4 \ldots$$

When numbers in a sequence are added together, the result is called a 'series':

$$\tfrac{1}{2} + \tfrac{1}{4} + \tfrac{1}{8} + \tfrac{1}{16} \ldots$$

This series is making its way towards the number 1. Adding the first two terms gives $\tfrac{3}{4}$, adding the next, $\tfrac{1}{8}$, to $\tfrac{3}{4}$ gives $\tfrac{7}{8}$. Then $\tfrac{7}{8} + \tfrac{1}{16} = \tfrac{15}{16}$, and so on.

A Rat's Life

Series and sequences occur in the real world, too. For instance, the number of rats after a certain number of generations is given by a series. Rats usually have about ten babies in each litter. The numbers in each generation are given by multiplying the number in the last generation by ten:

$$1, 10, 100, 1,000 \ldots$$

The total number of rats after the great-grandkids are born is:

$$1 + 10 + 100 + 1,000 = 1,111$$

The number in each generation can be obtained just by adding a zero to the last number, so in the 10th rat generation there would be 1,000,000,000 rats. Scary, eh? This sort of thing leads to some big numbers fast, which goes to show that you have to be careful in applying maths to the world – in this case, the assumption is that each baby rat survives to bear a litter of little rats, but in reality, not all of them will make it and breed, thank goodness.

The Fibonacci Sequence

Another sequence that can be applied in nature is known as the 'Fibonacci sequence'. It goes like this:

$$1, 1, 2, 3, 5, 8, 13, 21, 34 \ldots$$

There is a simple rule to make this sequence. Can you see what it is? (The answer is at the bottom of the page.)

This sequence turns up in some odd places. The pineapples on page 19 have two consecutive Fibonacci numbers in their spirals, and they are also found in the way that tree branches grow, the arrangements of seeds in sunflower heads, and the number of honeybees in successive generations.

Fibonacci numbers: add the most recent number to the one before it to get the next number in the sequence.

Patterns In Pences

You might even have Fibonacci numbers in your pocket.

If you have any 5-pence and 10-pence pieces, how many ways can you make 15 pence? You could have:

A 5 pence and   A 10 pence and   Three 5-pence
a 10 pence   a 5 pence   pieces

So there are three ways to make 15 pence. What about 20 pence? You could have:

Four 5-pence pieces   A 10 pence, a 5 pence   A 5 pence, a 10 pence
                 and a 5 pence   and a 5 pence

A 5 pence, a 5 pence   A 10 pence
and a 10 pence   and a 10 pence

So there are five ways to make 20 pence with 5 and 10-pence pieces. And, you've guessed it, there are eight ways to get 25 pence, 13 ways to get 30 pence and 21 ways to get 35 pence. How cool is that?

SIMPLY ENORMOUS

The Universe is utterly enormous. Just a single drop of water contains about ten billion trillion atoms, or 10,000,000,000,000,000,000,000,000. If you think that's plenty, the number of atoms in the ocean is about a trillion trillion times more than this. Not surprisingly, mathematicians have come up with a far easier way of showing these huge numbers. For example, a trillion trillion is written as 10^{24} which means '10 to the power of 24' or '10 multiplied by itself 24 times', or 1 followed by 24 zeros. This is called 'scientific notation'.

The Complex Googolplex

Some very large numbers have special names. For example, 10^{100} is a 'googol' – the name suggested by nine-year-old Milton Sirotta, in 1938. That's not all – there's also the 'googolplex', which is 10 to the power of a googol, or $10^{10^{100}}$.

That 'Sands' A Lot

The first person to study huge numbers was an ancient Greek, Archimedes. In his work *The Sand Reckoner,* he estimated the size of the Universe and how many grains of sand it would take to fill it. He took a 'myriad', the largest number in use at the time – 10,000 – and, by multiplying it by itself again and again, calculated that the whole Universe contained 8×10^{63} grains of sand. Since the Universe is quite possibly infinite, he was a way off, but it was still impressive work for the time.

BEYOND INFINITY

Imagine a number line (like the ones on pages 14 and 15), then imagine it extends for ever in both directions. This is 'infinity'. There is no largest number, because you can always add one more to make a bigger number.

In many ways, infinity is similar to zero, which cannot be divided. For example, half of infinity is infinity, and even a trillionth of infinity is still always infinity.

Infinitely Complicated

So does infinity mean anything? Well, it might, because you might live in an infinite Universe. If that's true, there may be an infinite number of stars. If just one in a trillion stars had a planet similar to Earth orbiting it, that would mean there would be an infinite number of planets like Earth, because a trillionth of infinity is infinity. If there are an infinite number of planets like Earth, there must be an infinite number of planets with humans living on them, and an infinite number of those humans must have your name, your age, your parents – there must be an infinite number of people just like you. It's enough to make your head spin!

I TOLD YOU WE'D GONE THE WRONG WAY – WE PASSED OUR EARTH TWO GALAXIES BACK.

STARTLING SHAPES

ALL KINDS OF SHAPES

A lot of mathematics is about simplifying things, from human behaviour to the motions of the planets. 'Geometry' – the mathematics of shapes – is no exception.

Natural Wonders

Many things in nature, such as trees or humans, for example, have complicated, irregular shapes that take a lot of describing.

Regular shapes don't occur naturally very often, but there are some, such as the disc of the Sun, or the hexagonal shapes of honeycomb in a beehive. In honeycomb, each cell is hexagonal. This maximizes the space in each one while keeping the gaps between them to a minimum.

If circles were used, more wax would be needed to fill the gaps between the cells. Isn't nature clever?

I DON'T CARE WHAT YOU DID IN YOUR LAST HIVE – WE USE HEXAGONS.

Where's Polly Gone?

Simple, regular shapes can be divided into shapes made of straight lines, such as squares, and shapes made of curves, such as circles. Straight-line shapes are called polygons.

Those with sides of equal length are called 'regular polygons'. These include:

The equilateral triangle

The square

The pentagon

The hexagon

The heptagon

The octagon

The nonagon

The decagon

After the square, the names of polygons settle down into a regular pattern. Each shape has the Greek word for the corresponding number of sides, followed by '-gon' – the Greek word for 'angle'.

TERRIFIC TRIANGLES

Other than circles, triangles are probably the shapes that mathematicians love best. So much so that the study of triangles has its own name: 'trigonometry'.

The Strongest Shape

The triangle is one of the simplest shapes because it has the smallest number of straight lines – and maths is all about simplifying. It is also one of the most useful shapes for building structures. In wet climates, many roofs are 'pitched', or triangular, so that the rain can run off easily. Cranes, bridges, and many other structures, are made of triangles, too. The reason is simple – it's the strongest shape.

Triangle Types

Triangles can be grouped into three kinds. These are:

Equilateral triangle
All three sides and all three angles are equal.

Isosceles triangle
Two sides and two angles are equal.

Scalene triangle
No sides and no angles are equal.

The three angles of the corners inside a triangle always add up to 180°, no matter what type it is.

Did You Know?

Angles of less than 90° are 'acute angles'. Angles of between 90° and 180° are known as 'obtuse angles' and those between 180° and 360° are 'reflex angles'.

Similar Triangles

If you wanted to find the height of something very tall, you'd need a long ladder and a huge tape measure, right?

Wrong. All you need to do is find a long, straight stick and something to measure – a nice, tall tree, for example. Push the stick into the ground a little way from the tree. Next, find a position on the ground where the top of the tree lines up with the top of the stick from your point of view. This will make two triangles – one from your eye to the stick and the one from your eye to the tree. They both have the same angles, even though they are different sizes. These are known as similar triangles.

8 metres

2 metres

The lengths of each side of similar triangles are also in proportion. With a few simple measurements, you can use this to work out the tree's height compared to the stick.

To do this, you need to measure the distance from A to D and the distance from A to B. Then divide the length of AB by the length of AD to get the ratio, which would be 4 in the example above. By multiplying the height of the stick by this ratio, you can find out the height of the tree.

In this case, $4 \times 1.5 = 6$, so the tree must be 6 metres tall – and all without going up a wobbly ladder!

Out of This World

Some distances are even trickier to measure directly – the distance to the Moon, for example – but triangles can still be used to calculate them. All you need to do is measure the length of one side of an imaginary triangle, between points A and B, to get a baseline. Then measure the angles made by the imaginary lines to the Moon at A and B. Since the Earth and Moon are both moving, this must be done at the same time, when the Moon is between the two. Once you know those angles, the length of lines AC and BC can be worked out, which also gives you the distance to the Moon. This process is called 'triangulation'.

Reach for the Stars

If you tried to triangulate a star using the same baseline as above, it would be too narrow because stars are so distant. There's a clever trick to increase the triangle's size though.

By measuring angle A first, then angle B six months later – when Earth is directly opposite in its orbit – the distance between points A and B will be double Earth's distance to the Sun. Using this interstellar-sized triangle, you can work out the distance to the star. Simple!

ALL ABOUT AREA

Simple, regular polygons, such as squares or rectangles, are easy when it comes to calculating 'area' – the amount of space they take up. Just multiply the length by the width. For a square measuring 4cm by 4cm, you simply multiply 4 x 4. The answer is 16, so the square has an area of 16cm². A rectangle that is 4cm by 2 cm has an area of 8cm².

Equally, if you want to know the distance around the edge of your square or rectangle – its 'perimeter' – you just combine the lengths of all four sides. How would you measure a circle though? There are no sides for you to multiply, and sometimes, it would be really useful to be able to work out a circle's area or 'circumference', which is the special name for the perimeter of a circle.

As Easy As Pi

The answer is a lot simpler than you may think. For centuries, people knew that for any circle, the circumference is just over three times the diameter – the distance across the middle of a circle. This ratio stays the same, whatever the size of the circle:

D   D   D

D Diameter

As time went on, people improved the calculation and, in fact, the circumference of a circle is more like 3.141592654 times the diameter. This number is called 'pi', which can also be written with this symbol: 'π' and is often abbreviated to 3.142. It is another irrational number (see pages 16 and 22), and actually goes on for ever.

The Area of a Circle

The way to work out the area of a circle involves pi again, but this time working with the radius, which is half the diameter. You just need a special formula: πr^2, or 'pi R squared', which means the area of a circle is equal to pi × (radius × radius). For example, if a circle had a radius of 4cm, the radius squared is 16. If you multiply π by this number, you get the area of the circle: $\pi \times 16 = 50.272\text{cm}^2$.

To look at the area of a circle in a more visual way, try cutting up a circle of paper, like this:

1. Fold your circle in half, then in half again crossways, dividing it into quarters, as shown.

2. Now fold the creases so that they meet and press down. Repeat at a right angle to this fold. Your circle will now be divided into eight equal segments.

3. Cut up the segments and lay four of them out in a row.

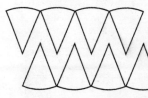

4. Slot the other four segments in to make a slightly bumpy, wonky rectangle called a 'parallelogram', with the same area as the circle.

The long side of this parallelogram measures the same as $\pi \times r$, the height is the same as r. To put it another way, $\pi \times r \times r$, or πr^2.

The more equal segments you cut your circle into, the more it will look like a rectangle.

INTO THE THIRD DIMENSION

Flat shapes, such as triangles, squares and rectangles, can be combined in various ways to make 3-dimensional shapes, or 'polyhedrons'. For example, a cube is made with six squares – a cuboid can be made up of three pairs of rectangles.

What's Inside?

The amount of space these shapes contain is called the 'volume'. You can easily find the volume of a cube or cuboid by multiplying its length, width and height together.

For example, to find the volume of a cube with edges that are 3cm long, you just multiply 3 by itself and then by itself again: $3 \times 3 \times 3$. So, 3×3 is 9, and 9×3 is 27, which means the cube has a volume of

27cm³, or 27 cubic centimetres.

A cuboid with sides of 2, 3 and 5 centimetres will have a volume of $2 \times 3 \times 5$, which is 30 cm³.

Simple Cylinders

People usually think of a cylinder as being shaped like a can of soup. However, the 'faces' (surfaces) can be any shape, as long as the cylinder has the same cross-section along its height.

If the faces at the ends of the cylinder are parallel, the volume will always be the area of the cross-section multiplied by the height.

To find the volume of a circular cylinder, you need the formula $\pi r^2 h$ – that's the formula for finding the area of a circle from page 41 multiplied by height, or 'h'. So a circular cylinder that is 5cm tall with faces that have a radius of 3cm would have a volume of $\pi \times 3 \times 3 \times 5$, which is 141.372cm^3.

Spherically Speaking

Humans might like shapes such as cuboids, but nature prefers the sphere – the most regular shape possible – for stars, planets as well as moons, bubbles, eyeballs and atoms. This is because a sphere uses the least possible surface area to enclose the maximum volume.

To find the volume of a sphere, you need to know the radius – the measurement from the exact centre of the sphere to its edge. To find the volume, you must cube the radius, multiply this number by 4π and then divide it by 3. This formula is usually written as $\frac{4}{3}\pi r^3$. For example, a sphere with a radius of 3cm will have a volume $27 \times \frac{1}{3} \times \pi$ or 36π, which is 113.097cm^3.

Shapes And Space

There are just five 3-dimensional shapes that have equal sides, equal angles and equal faces. These are known as 'regular polyhedrons', or 'platonic solids'. The ancient Greeks were very keen on geometrical shapes – in fact, they were so keen on platonic solids, they believed that they could be used to explain how the Universe was constructed.

The ancient Greeks believed that everything on Earth was made from four 'elements': earth, fire, water and air. They also thought that each one was made up of atoms shaped like one of the platonic solids, like this:

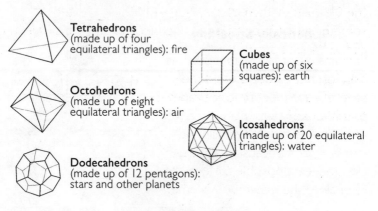

Tetrahedrons
(made up of four equilateral triangles): fire

Cubes
(made up of six squares): earth

Octohedrons
(made up of eight equilateral triangles): air

Icosahedrons
(made up of 20 equilateral triangles): water

Dodecahedrons
(made up of 12 pentagons): stars and other planets

Terrific Topology

To study shapes that are more complex than regular polyhedrons, 'topology' is used.

Topology studies what happens to shapes when you squash, stretch or twist them. When shapes can be stretched or twisted to make another shape, they can be described as 'topologically equivalent'. For example, a doughnut and a needle can be described as topologically equivalent, because they both have a hole going through them. Neither can be described as topologically equivalent to a glass, however, as a glass does not have a hole going through it.

Mind-Bending Möbius

Topologists have made some rather weird discoveries about shapes. For instance, 3-dimensional objects are thought of as having an inside and an outside, but, in 1858, the German mathematician, August Möbius, created something that had just one continuous surface. It is known as the 'Möbius strip'.

You can make your own Möbius strip quite easily. Take a strip of paper, twist it once and stick the ends together so that it looks like this:

Take a pen and draw a line along the middle of the strip without lifting it off the paper. Your pen will cover every bit of the strip, then come back round to meet your starting point, proving that the Möbius strip has just one surface.

Baffling Bottles

A man named Felix Klein came up with an even more incredible idea. The bottle named after him is a shape with just one side – a continuous one-sided cylinder, in a way. In fact, a true Klein bottle would be 4-dimensional, as it needs to pass through itself without making a hole, which is impossible in three dimensions.

INNER SPACE

The Klein bottle on the previous page is an example of a 4-dimensional model – well, a 3-dimensional model of a 4-dimensional shape, but what does that actually mean?

A shape with no dimensions looks like this ...   ... well, like nothing, really. 0-dimensional shapes occupy no space, so there's nothing to see.

The First Three Dimensions

One-dimensional shapes can't really be seen either, as they are just lines with no thickness. However, in mathematics, it's normal to imagine that lines are just thick enough to allow them to be drawn. So, here is a one-dimensional shape:

By extending it sideways, you can make a 2-dimensional shape. Here it is as a diamond, or 'rhombus':

If you add some vertical lines and another rhombus, it becomes a representation of a 3-dimensional shape – a 'rhomboid'.

What about the fourth dimension – how would that look?

46

Into the Fourth Dimension!

To look at the fourth dimension and beyond, imagine a square. A 2-dimensional square is made with four lines – a 3-dimensional cube is made with 12 lines. The next square shape – in the fourth dimension – has 32 lines and is known as a 'tesseract', or 'hypercube'.

The best way to think of a tesseract is to imagine two 3-dimensional cubes attached to each other, so that every face of the cube becomes a 3-dimensional shape, like this:

Did You Know?

Time is also a dimension. You travel from morning to night, just as you travel to and from school. Although, of course, reversing, turning and stopping in time isn't possible – yet!

Spacetime

Time and space are always linked – they are known as 'spacetime'. The most famous scientist to work with spacetime was Albert Einstein. He discovered that when things travel very quickly, they change shape.

Imagine that there was a big bomb travelling through space. Einstein proved that if it was going fast enough, it would change shape, like this:

How Special!

Another part of Einstein's spacetime theories said that time passes at different rates depending on how the person measuring it is moving. If you were unfortunate enough to be on the bomb, you might measure the time for its fuse to burn down as a minute. If someone on the ground watched you whiz past and timed the fuse, too, they might measure it as taking two minutes. To look at it another way, imagine a spaceship travelling at nearly the speed of light. If the astronauts on board travelled for what they measured as a year, they would find that far longer had passed on Earth when they returned to it – perhaps thousands of years.

An Extra Dimension or Three

Does the world really just have four dimensions? Of course not, that would be silly. In reality scientists think it has 11!

'M-theory' – the idea of 11 dimensions – suggests that ten dimensions are of space and one is time.

How come no one has ever noticed all these extra dimensions though? The answer is that they are scrunched up too small to see, or 'compactified'. Perhaps this is just as well – a 10-dimensional equivalent of a cube, called a 'dekeract', is made up of 5,120 lines – imagine that!

Did You Know?

Einstein's theories also say that the speed of light is the fastest thing possible. Until very recently, everyone was still certain that was true. However, scientists in Switzerland, at the European Organization for Nuclear Research, or CERN for short, discovered that it might be possible for tiny particles, called 'neutrinos', to move faster.

PERFECT SYMMETRY

Many shapes, and other things, too, have 'symmetry', which means that if you were to cut them in half from top to bottom, the two halves would be similar, if not identical.

Even people have symmetry. If you were to draw a line down the middle of your body, from the top of your head to your feet, the two halves would be very similar. The line you drew down yourself is called an 'axis of symmetry'.

How Many Axes?

Many regular shapes have several axes of symmetry. This square, for instance, has four axes of symmetry. Can you work out how many axes of symmetry a circle has? The answer is at the bottom of the page.

Mirror, Mirror

MIRROR, MIRROR, ON THE WALL, WHO IS THE MOST SYMMETRICAL OF THEM ALL?

Take a mirror and hold it at a 90 ° angle against a photo of your face, so that it goes straight down the middle of your nose and chin. You will see a whole face in the mirror and it will be exactly symmetrical. Turn the mirror and repeat it with the other side of your face. Do the images look similar or different? The more similar the images are, the more symmetrical your face is.

A circle has an infinite number of axes of symmetry.

MATHEMATICAL STRUCTURES

Man-made structures come in many shapes and sizes. Some are pleasing to the eye, while others seem completely ugly. Part of the reason why some look more appealing can be summed up mathematically.

The Golden Ratio

The United Nations building in New York and the Parthenon in Athens both have the same ratio of length to height: 1:1.618. This is known as the 'golden ratio'. It can also be represented by the Greek letter 'phi' or 'Φ' (not to be confused with pi!). As well as cropping up in architecture, it also pops up in art.

The golden ratio has some interesting mathematical properties, too. If you take a rectangle with a golden ratio like the one below and divide it into a square and another rectangle, the smaller rectangle will also have the golden ratio. This can be repeated again and again.

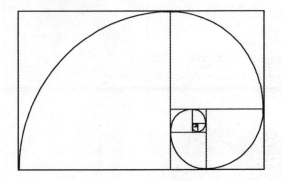

What's more, if you draw a curve between opposite corners of each square, you will create a spiral.

THE ART OF MATHS

The further away things are from you, the smaller they appear to be. The basic rule is that if something is twice as far away, it appears to be half the width and height. For artists, learning how to draw or paint things in 'perspective' – so that they look the right size – is an important skill.

The Point of Vanishing Points

Imagine standing in the middle of a straight, flat road. The sides of the road would seem to get closer together the further away they were until they looked as though they joined in a point. In art, this is called the 'vanishing point'.

Putting It in Perspective

If you look at any painting created before the 15th century, you'll probably find it looks rather odd – artists hadn't really mastered the art of perspective yet.

Vanishing point

Horizon line

If you are drawing a picture that has lots of parallel lines – a straight, flat road lined with houses, for instance, all the objects will disappear to the same vanishing point. This means you can draw in guidelines to help you check that your perspective looks right.

MUSIC BY NUMBERS

Maths is very useful for music, too. In fact, it's numbers that make the difference between music and a terrible din.

Here's what happens when you strum or pluck the string of an instrument like a guitar:

When you strum a guitar, for instance, the vibrating string makes this kind of shape.

If you press your finger halfway along its length, its shape changes to this.

When you do this, the sound that the string produces rises in pitch, so that it sounds higher, but it still sounds similar.

In music, these two notes are connected with the same letter name – C, for example. These two C-notes are described as an 'octave' apart – an interval of eight notes: C, D, E, F, G, A, B and C. An interval is the distance from one note to another.

The sounds that the string makes are actually waves, a little like the ripples you see when a pebble is dropped in a pond, except that they are travelling in all directions through the air.

Perfect Harmony

Notes that are in harmony sound good together because they make simple ratios. In notes an octave apart, the ratio is two to one. The higher-pitched note has a wavelength that is exactly half as long as the other, which makes sense if you remember it is produced by halving the length of the string.

When two notes an octave apart are played together, they sound good. Other combinations sound good, too. For example, an interval of a fifth is a pair of notes where one has a wavelength one-and-a-half times as long as the other. Notes that sound unpleasant together have different wavelengths, which clash, because they don't make simple ratios – just like the sound they produce.

Pythagoras and Planets

Your old friend, Pythagoras (see pages 20 to 21), first noticed that the pleasant or harsh sounds that different combinations of notes made involved ratios. Pythagoras was so set on his ratios idea that he thought the entire Universe could be explained with numbers. He and his followers believed that the distances between planets were simple ratios and that they made harmonious sounds as they moved. This idea was called the 'music of the spheres' and was popular for many centuries.

TURN THAT
NOISE DOWN!

A MATTER OF DEGREES

According to many people – especially everyone who has to go up it – Baldwin Street, in Dunedin, New Zealand, is the steepest street in the world. This has been subject to much discussion, largely because there are so many ways to measure its 'gradient' – or steepness.

How Is It Measured?

Steepness can be measured using a ratio. Baldwin Street's ratio is 1: 2.86. This means for every 2.86 metres travelled horizontally, the street rises by 1 metre.

Percentages are sometimes used to measure a gradient instead. Baldwin Street's gradient is 35 %, which means that for every metre travelled, the street rises by 35 cm.

The gradient can also be expressed as an angle in degrees, known as an 'angle of elevation' – the amount that it rises from an imaginary horizontal position on the ground. Baldwin Street's angle of elevation is 19.3 °.

SCALING THE HEIGHTS

Old science-fiction films were full of giant, killer insects and other monsters, but why are they so small in real life? The answer is mathematical, of course.

An Ant Experiment

Insects, such as ants, don't have a skeleton like you. Instead, their hard outer shells, or exoskeletons, support their bodies. An insect also breathes through its 'exoskeleton', but there is a limit to how much air it can absorb. That amount depends on the insect's surface area. However, the amount of air an insect needs depends on its volume. The problem is that volume and area don't get bigger at the same rate. Look at the table below to see what would happen if an ant became 10cm long, or even 100cm long:

Ant Size	Length (cm)	Surface Area (cm²)	Volume (cm³)
Small	1	1	1
Large	10	100	1,000
Giant	100	10,000	1,000,000
Monster	1,000	1,000,000	1,000,000,000

The small ant's volume and area are fine – it can absorb as much air as it needs through its exoskeleton. However, as the size of the ant increases, the volume increases far more than the surface area. By the time the ant is monster-sized, its volume is a thousand times its surface area. This means that the ant couldn't possibly have a large enough surface area to provide the oxygen its body would need. (See pages 42 to 43 for more on volume.)

Sizing Things Up

Look at this picture of an elephant shrew and an elephant. Even though they look the same size here, you know automatically that the shrew is far smaller than the elephant. What if an alien mathematician looked at them though?

Surprisingly, the alien would probably know that, too. This is because of the shrew's tiny legs. They are too thin in proportion to its body compared to the elephant's legs.

Don't Fall!

When something falls – an elephant, say – the air pushes back up against it. This force, called 'resistance', depends on the falling object's area, but the force downwards depends on its weight. The object's weight depends on its volume, which also depends on how dense* it is. The smaller the object, the more air-resistance there is per kilogram, which means it is slowed more than a larger object would be.

This means that if you were unlucky enough to fall from a height of 4 metres, you'd have to go to hospital. A spider would hardly notice, while an elephant … well, don't worry about giant ants, but do watch out for falling elephants!

* Density relates to mass – an object the size of a ping-pong ball, but made of iron, would have more density than an object the same size made of cheese.

MEASURING MONARCHS

Not so long ago, people didn't measure in metres and centimetres. In fact, quite a different approach was taken. Some measurements were based on body parts, which is why the height of horses is still measured in 'hands' and, sometimes, the height of people is given in 'feet' and 'inches'.

Handy Measurements

In ancient Egypt, things were measured in something called 'cubits', which was the length of the current pharaoh's forearm, plus a hand width. The length was carved into a granite block, and wooden or stone copies were given to builders. This worked fine, but only for as long as the pharaoh lived. Lengths were likely to change as pharaohs came and went, which was probably quite annoying if you were half-way through building something.

There were also a dozen different lengths, that were all called cubits, known to have been used in the ancient world, which must have been very confusing.

Inching Forwards

Over the next few centuries, many measuring systems were used around the world, and these could vary within countries. In Britain, for example, it wasn't until the 13th century that people tried to standardize measurements across the country, when it was ruled that an inch was the length of three barleycorns. Over time, Britain adopted the imperial system of inches, feet (12 inches), yards (3 feet) and miles (1,760 yards). This remained until it was gradually replaced by the metric system of centimetres, metres and kilometres, but who decided you should all use that?

CURIOUS UNITS

In 1960, an international system of units of measurement was formally agreed. They are called SI units, which stands for *Système International* – French for 'International System'.

Incredible Seven

There are seven standard SI units. There's the metre for distance, the kilogram for mass and the second for time. Then there's the ampere for electric current, the kelvin for temperature, the mole for an amount of substance, and the candela for luminous intensity, or brightness of things. These units are used as a jumping-off point for all other types of metric unit.

What's more, even though there are so many sorts of things that you might want to measure – such as loudness, cloudiness, smoothness and sharpness – the seven SI units can measure them all, thanks to mathematics.

Really Big, or Really Small?

What happens if you want to measure something huge or something tiny using SI units? After all, metres are particularly good for measuring the height of a tree, but probably not so good for measuring the size of its leaves. And, if you want to measure the size of a whole forest, you're likely to need something far larger.

Which Unit Is Best?

By using the seven main SI units as a starting point, you can scale each type of unit up or down to measure all sorts of things. All you do is add a different 'prefix', or beginning, to the words to indicate that a larger or smaller measurement is being used. For example, the 'kilo-' part of kilometre means 'one thousand', the 'centi-' part of centimetre means 'one hundredth' and the 'milli-' part of millimetre means 'one thousandth'.

If you wanted, you could measure distance travelled in centimetres, but it would be quite tricky for a motorist to know which turning to take. Instead, it's best to try to choose the most suitable measurement for the thing you are measuring.

... CONTINUE STRAIGHT FOR 100,000 CENTIMETRES AND YOU WILL REACH YOUR DESTINATION.

Red-Faced on the Red Planet

SI units have been adopted by most countries around the world. This means that when people are working with other nations to build things, everyone is working from the same set of measurements. That may not seem so important, but when no one is sure which unit of measurement is being used, the results can be chaotic, with very expensive consequences!

For instance, in 1999, NASA's Mars Climate Orbiter, which cost $125 million to build, had successfully completed nearly all of its journey. It was on its final approach to the Martian atmosphere … and that's where things went wrong. One team was working in old-fashioned imperial units, while the other was working in metric. The result was that the orbit was miscalculated and the Orbiter crashed. How embarrassing!

PRECISELY ACCURATE

The words 'accurate' and 'precise' might sound as though they can be used interchangeably. In reality, they have slightly different meanings.

Right on Target!

An archer has shot five arrows into each target below:

Precise, but   Accurate, but   Precise and
not accurate   not precise   accurate.

On the first target, all the arrows are close together, so the archer has managed high precision. However, they are not near the centre of the target, so his accuracy is low.

On the second target, the archer has achieved a high level of accuracy, as all the arrows are close to the centre of the target. In this case though, his level of precision is low as the arrows aren't close to each other.

As you can see, on the final target, the archer has shot the arrows both accurately and precisely.

'GUESSTIMATION'

Being able to estimate is a useful skill and one that most humans are rather good at. For example, did you know that when trying to judge whether something is at a right-angle or not, most humans can spot errors of less than a degree?

The ability to estimate can also help with everyday things, such as crossing a road. By estimating the speed and distance of vehicles, you can judge whether or not you have enough time to cross a road safely.

I'M SURE THERE'S ENOUGH TIME TO ... BLEURGH!

TOO FAST!

However, people don't think in terms of units naturally. Rather than thinking, 'That car is moving at about 20 kilometres an hour,' you are more likely to think in terms of, 'That's too fast,' or, 'There's enough time to cross.'

Simple Samples

Estimating can save time, too. For instance, you might be asked to find out the type and number of different creatures living in the turf of a playing field. Counting them all would take a ridiculous amount of time. Instead, you could estimate the answer using a process called sampling.

To sample an area, the first thing that's needed is a 'quadrat' – a square made of four rods joined together, each a metre long. This is placed on the playing field, then all the living creatures found in that area are collected and recorded. For example, you might find 4 earthworms, 16 ants, 3 beetles and 1 slug.

Now, say that the playing field measures 100 by 70 metres. If you multiply these figures together, you can find out the playing field's area: $100 \times 70 = 7,000$ m^2.

To estimate how many creatures there are, simply multiply the numbers of the quadrat populations by 7,000 to give:

AAARGH!

> 28,000 earthworms,
> 112,000 ants,
> 21,000 beetles,
> 7,000 slugs.

Of course, this type of approach has to be used with care. If you happened to find a coin in the square, too, it's very unlikely that there would be a fortune scattered across the rest of the field.

Surprising Guesses

Making estimates can lead to some amazing facts, and even to some disturbing ones. For example, Shakespeare's dying breath in 1616 would probably have contained around 1,000,000,000,000,000,000,000 air molecules. Over the next four centuries, these molecules have spread across the world and through the atmosphere, which contains about 1,000,000,000,000,000,000,000,000,000,000,000,000,000,000 air molecules (that's a million, billion, billion, billion, billion).

If you divide the larger number by the smaller one, you get 1,000,000,000,000,000,000,000. This means that you can estimate that 1 in every 1,000,000,000,000,000,000,000 molecules in the air is from Shakespeare's last breath. However, this also happens to be the same number of molecules you breathe in every breath, so there's a good chance that your next breath includes a molecule from Shakespeare's last one!

These enormous numbers are too big for a calculator, but there is a quick way to work with them. As you know from page 32, long numbers such as 1,000 can be expressed as powers of 10, so 1,000 can be written as 10^3 – because it is the same as $10 \times 10 \times 10$. The number of molecules in Shakespeare's last breath can be shortened to 10^{21}. The number of molecules in the atmosphere is 10^{42}.

Handily, dividing these numbers gives the same answer as subtracting their powers of 10. So the question above can also be worked out as $10^{42} \div 10^{21}$ which is 10^{21}.

A Calculated Guess

Estimation can also be useful when using calculators and spreadsheets to work things out. This is because if you have a rough idea of how much the total will be, it's much easier to spot when a mistake has been made, so that you can check if the wrong button has been pressed.

FOOLING YOURSELF

The fact that the human brain can estimate all sorts of things means it needs to make assumptions. For example, you might spot a dot on the horizon that gets bigger until you see a tiny person. If that person gets larger, you would assume that they were approaching you, and that they were about your size. Once these assumptions are made, your brain can use the laws of perspective (see page 52), to judge the distance of the person and their speed of approach.

The problem with assumptions is that they can sometimes be wrong, which can result in an optical illusion, like this:

Your brain will try to make the best sense it can of what you are looking at.

At first, it might seem as though you're looking at an image of a box seen from above. However, after a while, a different perspective might be seen of a box viewed from below. Which one is correct?

Either is correct. The image of the box is an optical illusion known as a Necker Cube. The human brain tries to make sense of it when really there isn't enough information, which is why you can see two perspectives.

NAILING DOWN MOTION

In maths and physics, there are two types of measurements called 'scalars' and 'vectors'. A scalar quantity is simply a number that can increase or decrease. A vector is a number that can increase or decrease, but that also has a direction.

The speed of a car – 20 kilometres per hour, or km/h, for example – is a scalar quantity, meaning it can only go up or down. However, the 'velocity' of a car is a vector. This is because velocity is speed in a particular direction – say, 20 km/h south.

A Plane's Progress

If a plane were to fly from London to Los Angeles – a distance of about 8,800km – in 10 hours, at what velocity would it need to fly? Logically, you might think it should be 880km/h west, but what if the wind was blowing towards it at 100km/h?

Travelling at 880km/h through the air

West

Wind = 100km/h

Plane travelling 780km/h above the ground

East

Los Angeles

London

Flying into a wind slows things down, so to make the calculation you need to subtract the wind velocity from the plane velocity:

$$880 - 100 = 780\text{km/h west.}$$

That's also why a plane can sometimes arrive sooner than expected – if the wind is behind it, the velocity increases.

The First True Scientist

Much of the early work related to motion was carried out 400 years ago by the Italian scientist Galileo Galilei. In many ways, Galileo was the first true scientist in that he tried to explain the Universe and the laws that describe what happens in it with the aid of numbers.

The Law of Falling Bodies

Galileo realized that Earth's gravity pulls everything downwards, which is why, if things are free to move, they will fall. As they do, the Earth keeps pulling, making them go faster and faster.

One of Galileo's real strokes of genius was to realize that the presence of air on Earth affects the way things move. In reality, falling objects reach a steady velocity after a while, called 'terminal velocity'. This is because the drag of the air on them stops them speeding up any further, which is why feathers fall more slowly than cannonballs. If you were to drop a feather and a cannonball on the Moon, where there is no air, they would fall at the same rate.

By imagining how things would fall if there were no air, Galileo recognized that the laws of falling objects were very simple. He realized that they could be described with some quite straightforward mathematics:

> Objects fall with a steady, or 'constant' acceleration. So, if an object is falling at a particular velocity, after 1 second it will be falling twice as fast; after 2 seconds, 3 times as fast; after 3 seconds, 4 times as fast, and so on.

What's more:

> If an object has fallen through a particular distance in 1 second, it will have fallen through a total of 4 times that distance after 2 seconds, 9 times the distance after 3 seconds and 16 times the distance after 4 seconds.

Have you noticed how the two sets of numbers are related? The distances – 1, 4, 9 and 16 – are the squares of the times – 1, 2, 3 and 4. The longer an object falls, the faster it travels.

Did You Know?

You might wonder what the point of these ideas and discoveries is if air resistance means they don't apply. Well, on Earth, adjustments can be made to mathematical equations to take this into account. And if you travelled into space, you'd soon find them useful – spacecraft obey these rules because there is no air to slow them down.

BLINK AND YOU'LL MISS IT

The briefest moments of time are measured in less than a trillionth of a trillionth of a trillionth of a 'nanosecond' (billionth of a second). A nanosecond is so quick that it takes 100 million nanoseconds to blink just once, so it is not a measurement that is particularly useful for everyday life.

I MISSED THAT LAST 100 MILLION, SORRY – I BLINKED.

Only A Matter Of Time

You might not spot a nanosecond easily, but time is something that you are probably very aware of. Whether it's minutes dragging by during a dull lesson, or hours whizzing past as you enjoy an over-too-soon birthday. What is time exactly though, and how is it measured?

Early humans would measure time passing in various ways – including the changing of the seasons, or the shape of the Moon over the course of a month. Eventually however, people wanted more accurate ways to measure time. To do this, they came up with some useful units to measure it.

Minute After Minute

You already know that there are 60 seconds in a minute and 60 minutes in an hour, and that there are 24 hours in a day, seven days in a week and 365 days in a year. Why is it that months don't follow a pattern though? Some have 30 days, others 31 or even 28 or 29. To find out why, you'll need to go back in time to see how it was first measured.

71

CLOCK THIS

One of the earliest ways to measure the passage of a day was developed in ancient Egypt around 3,500 years ago. The 'shadow clock', as it was called, relied on the shadow cast by the Sun as it moved across the sky. It worked because a shadow's length and direction change as the Sun moves.

Playing with Shadows

The shadow clock was quite simple and divided the hours of daylight into ten, plus an hour of twilight in the morning and one in the evening. It consisted of a raised bar that cast a shadow over another bar, along which 'hours' were marked. In the mornings, the raised bar pointed east, so that the shadow fell on the hour bar to the west. At noon, the clock would be rotated to point in the other direction, and follow the Sun as it moved from east to west. What's more, a shadow clock was portable, although it had to be aligned just right each time it was moved.

However, a shadow clock could not be used to tell the time at night, and, if the sky was cloudy during the day, you wouldn't have any idea if you were on right on time or super-late. Another problem was that the further away from the equator you were, the more the lengths of days differed throughout the year. This would mean that, in winter, your shadow clock would divide the day up into the same number of hours, but that they would be shorter.

Although no one is sure exactly where or when sundials were first used, they look much more like the circular clocks and watches you see now. They were a big improvement on shadow clocks, as the hours they measured were the same length throughout the year.

THE FACE DIVIDES THE DAY INTO 12 HOURS.

However, there was still the problem that they had to be properly aligned and relied on sunlight to show the time.

Clocks for Cloudy Days

What was needed was a clock that could measure time inside or out, whatever the weather, day or night.

The ancient Egyptians experimented with water clocks. The earliest surviving example dates from around 1500 BCE. These clocks worked by allowing water to drip at a steady rate into a bowl where the 'hours' were marked up the side. However, they still weren't very accurate.

Things finally improved with the invention of the mechanical clock sometime in the 14th century. It worked thanks to a gradually falling weight, which turned a system of gears. These clocks *still* weren't very accurate though.

What was really needed was something to make sure that the speed of the dropping weight was constant, so that the gears turned at a constant speed, too. Galileo (see page 111) is known to have sketched some ideas for a clock that used a pendulum in 1642, but the first was made by a man named Christiaan Huygens, in 1656. Its swinging pendulum made the clock the most accurate way of timekeeping until the 20th century.

Getting There!

In the 17th century, people knew the Earth rotated 360° in a day, and 15° an hour. If you sailed east for an hour, you knew that your location was 15° east of your starting point. If you were a few minutes out though, your location would be wrong. Pendulum clocks, although accurate on land, wouldn't work at sea. In 1759, John Harrison's 'H4', an over-sized, but accurate, pocket watch, solved this problem.

Meanwhile, on dry land, many clocks were set locally. When the Sun was directly overhead, it was noon, but this changes slightly from place to place, so time differed from town to town. In the 19th century, railway networks came along and a standard time, known as 'railway time', was brought in.

Get in the Zone

In 1884, the Royal Greenwich Observatory in London was chosen as the spot for the 'prime meridian'. This meant that the vertical lines of longitude on a map always started from 0° in Greenwich. It was also a handy spot as at midday in Greenwich, it was midnight on the other side of the planet in the middle of the Pacific Ocean. This meant that the fewest people possible would be affected by the change in date – along a line known as the International Date Line.

That's Atomic

The most accurate time instruments today rely on the regular vibrations of atoms. They are so accurate that one at the UK's National Physical Laboratory will lose or gain less than a second over the next 138 million years!

WHEN DAYS GO MISSING

Centuries ago, measuring the passage of a year was even more challenging than measuring the hours of the day. Many people relied on the Sun or the Moon to help them keep track of the days. In ancient Egypt, farmers based their calendar on the level of the river Nile. In ancient Rome, the army calendar used the lunar month – the time it took for the Moon to pass through all its phases. The year was then divided up into 13 phases.

THIS YEAR'S JUST FLYING BY.

None of these systems worked particularly well. For example, the Moon takes about 29 ½ days to go through its full cycle, so the Roman army's 13 cycles made 383 ½ days, as 13 x 29 ½ = 383 ½ days. This is longer than a true year, which is the time it takes the Earth to orbit the Sun – a solar year.

Around The Sun In Just Over 365 Days

Why was it so hard to divide a year up? The answer is that Earth orbits the Sun in 365 ¼ days, minus 11 minutes, so it can't be divided evenly. Over time, these extra ¼ days would build up, so that eventually your year would be so out of synch, you'd be celebrating New Year in the summer.

Calendar Chaos

The ancient Romans had been noting the problem for many years and, in 45 BCE, Emperor Julius Caesar reformed the calendar. The problem was that it completely messed up the year – days slipped so much that Caesar had an extra 90 days added to 46 BCE to correct the problem. No wonder it was called 'the Year of Confusion'!

Lovely Leap Years

To stop the problem happening again, the Romans decided to carry over the ¼ days at the end of each year, for three years. They then added an extra day at the end of every fourth year, so they were 366 days long. These are leap years. However, the calendar still wasn't right – the extra quarter-days were 11 minutes short! Over time, these 11 minutes built up again and by the mid-16th century, the calendar was ten days out.

So, in 1582, Pope Gregory announced that ten days would be missed out to make things right again. It was also ruled that a century year, such as 1600, 1700 and 1800, should not be a leap year unless it could be divided exactly by 400. In some countries this correction didn't happen until much later. For example, in Britain, the correction was done in 1752, when 11 days were missed out. It is said this prompted riots by some people complaining that the government had stolen 11 days of their lives!

NEVER MIND THE CALENDAR CHANGING – YOU FORGOT MY BIRTHDAY!

GETTING FROM A TO B

A calculation or a formula is all very well for lots of mathematical information, but, sometimes, a picture is

much more useful. Take directions, for instance. It's simple enough to say, 'Walk past Wishing Well Hill, through Bad Wolf Wood and on the other side is Grandma's House,' but what if you need to direct someone over a longer distance? It's easier to show this by drawing a map.

Sizing It Up

Drawing a map is better than nothing, but it doesn't tell you about the distances between things, or how big they are in relation to each other. What would be better is a map that is drawn 'to scale'.

This map has a scale, shown as a ratio, of 1:10,000. This means that 1cm on the map is equal to 10,000cm – or 100 metres – in the real world. You can use the scale on a map to help you calculate distances.

To work out distances in a straight line, all you need is a piece of paper. Mark off the length of the scale – in this case, 1cm – on your piece of paper, then place it on the map to work out the distances between places.
For example, it is 3.25cm between the Wicked Queen's Castle and Grandma's House – on the scale of 1:10,000, this is 32,500cm, or 325 metres.

If you want to measure a distance that isn't a straight line, you can use a piece of string to follow the curve of your route – around the base of Wishing Well Hill, for example. You can then measure the amount of string against the scale line on the map.

Scaling the Heights

Maps can even show how the land rises and falls, using what are called 'contour lines'. Map-makers take points on a hill or valley that are the same height and join them up in a series of rings. The rings show the shape and relative heights of hills and mountains, and the depths of valleys.

Steep slopes are shown on a map with lines that are close together, gentler while slopes have widely spaced lines. On this map, the hill rings showing Wishing Well Hill are quite close together, so it is probably quite steep – it might be better to go around it!

Which Way Up?

To be able to read a map, you also need to know about direction. This is shown with an arrow to mark north pointing towards the top of the map. By using the map with a compass, you can make sure you are going in the right direction. It's useful because it works in all conditions.

Groovy Grids

Most maps have horizontal and vertical 'grid lines' that match the scale. In this map, each square on the grid is 1cm wide. You know that the scale is 1:10,000, so you also know that each square represents 100 metres on the ground.

Grid lines help you to pinpoint an exact position by using a 'grid reference'. For example, you might ask your friends to meet you at 2317, but to find that exact spot, they'll need to know what the numbers mean. In this case, the first two numbers tell you how far *across* the map to look – the second two numbers tell you how far *up* the map to look.* Remind yourself with this useful saying:

Along the corridor and up the stairs.

Then everyone will know to meet on the riverbank north of Pirate Island – at the bottom left-hand corner of the square where lines 23 and 17 cross.

* The numbers across and the numbers up are sometimes known as 'eastings' and 'northings'.

X MARKS THE SPOT

You might need to pinpoint an even more exact location that lies between the grid lines – the Wicked Queen's Castle, for instance. In this case, you'll need to give a six-figure reference to help your friends to find it. The number 216205 tells you the exact location of the castle. The first two numbers tell you to go across the map to line 21 – the fourth and fifth numbers tell you to go up to line 20:

216205.

You then need to imagine each square is divided into 100 smaller squares, each 10 metres wide – ten across and ten up. The third number shows the exact horizontal position: 6. The sixth number shows the exact vertical position: 5.

the Wicked Queen's Castle

This tells you that the castle is 60 metres east and 50 metres north of the corner of square 2120.

Clever Co-ordinates

If you know the 'co-ordinates', or grid references, of two locations, then you can calculate the distance between them. In the map opposite, an explorer is shown at grid reference 212173 – and he wants to get to Grandma's House, which is at 252204.

To work out the distance between the two, you can draw a right-angled triangle over the map and use Pythagoras's theorem. This states that if the squares of the lengths of the two short sides are added, the result is the square of the length of the longest side, or hypotenuse. (See pages 20 to

21 for more on Pythagoras.) So to find the distance to Grandma's House – the long side of the triangle – you first have to work out the lengths of the two shorter sides.

Here, the horizontal line shows you how far east Grandma's House is from the explorer's current location. The explorer is 20 metres east of grid line 21 and the house is 20 metres east of grid line 25. Each square is equal to 100 metres on the ground, so the horizontal line, **A**, is 400 metres long.

The vertical line shows you how far north Grandma's House is from the explorer. He is 30 metres north of line 17 and the house is 40 metres north of grid line 20, so the vertical line, **B**, is 310 metres long.

Now you can apply Pythagoras's theorem:

$$400 \times 400 = 160,000 \text{ metres, and}$$
$$310 \times 310 = 96,100 \text{ metres.}$$

If $a^2 + b^2$ = the distance to Grandma's House squared, and these two figures added together make 256,100, then the house is approximately 500 metres from the explorer (there is a special square-root button on some calculators marked '$\sqrt{}$' to help you work this out!).

DRAMATIC DATA

GREAT GRAPHS

The easiest way to organize a lot of information, or 'data', can be to use a diagram. Diagrams can communicate data clearly and easily and make it easier to understand – they can even be used to predict future measurements.

There are many types of diagram that mathematicians use – graphs, bar charts, pie charts and Venn diagrams are just a few. It's important to choose the right type of diagram for the information, otherwise it won't make sense at all.

Plot It Out

A line graph can be used to plot information that changes over time. For example, this graph shows a boy's height from birth to the age of 18, plotted once a year:

The bottom-left corner marks the starting point for the horizontal scale – also known as the x-axis – and the vertical scale – also known as the y-axis.

By joining the dots each year, the pattern of growth from birth to when the boy reaches adulthood can be seen. It's clear that the boy grew rapidly in his first year, and that the rate of growth slowed as he neared 18.

Plotting The Future

In the line graph on the previous page, all the information you needed was included. What if you wanted to use a graph to try to find out what might happen next though?

For instance, imagine a car is travelling along a road and a passenger is recording the time every 200 metres. They might end up with a table looking something like this:

Distance (metres)	Time (seconds)
0	0
200	22
400	35
600	57
800	84
1,000	96
1,200	123

This information can be plotted on a graph with the time along the x-axis and the distance along the y-axis, like this:

The speed of the car is changing all the time, so instead of joining all the points, a 'best-fit' line has been drawn straight through as many points as possible. It gives you the car's average velocity (see pages 68 to 70).

You can use this best-fit line to work out how long it might take the car to travel 1,400 metres. On the graph, you'll see that the line shows that if the car continued to travel at the same average velocity, it would take 132 seconds to travel 1,400 metres.

Tracking Trends

Graphs can also look at what are called 'trends'. A trend is the general direction in which something is moving. This graph shows the average life expectancy of UK residents from 1960 until 2010 – over time, the trend is that life expectancy is increasing.

If you draw a best-fit line through the trend line, it will show an average for the increase in life expectancy.

In 1960, the average was 71 years – by 2010, it was just over 80 years. So, in 50 years, life expectancy increased by 9 years.

You can 'extrapolate'*, or predict, how the information might go on by extending the straight line to show the next 10 years. Shown here with a dotted line, you can see that by 2020, the average life expectancy should be around 81.

* It's important to be careful with extrapolation – if you did the same thing backwards, for example, with life expectancy decreasing by 9 years every 50 years, eventually, the average life expectancy would be zero!

Mistakes and Misunderstandings

Sometimes, data on a graph can seem a little odd. Here is one for 'Cure-O', a medicine that is meant to cure hiccups.

The first graph shows the best-fit line for the data. It seems to suggest that if you took 20 doses of Cure-O, you wouldn't get hiccups at all.

However, when you can see the individual doses, they are so widely scattered that there isn't really a trend at all.

In fact, if you take out one piece of data, the best-fit line changes, so it seems that the more Cure-O you take, the more hiccups you get!

This goes to show how important it is to analyse data very carefully.

It is easy to jump to conclusions once you start extrapolating, and that can lead to some strange results!

When you're plotting data on a graph, particularly if you are using computer software to add best-fit lines, make sure that your results seem logical!

A MEAN SET OF NUMBERS

Graphs are one way of grappling with data. They make up an area of mathematics called 'statistics', along with the methods below.

Averaging Out

If you catch a bus every day, one thing you might want to find out is how long the journey takes on average. The first thing you would have to do is note down how many minutes several journeys take. Your data might look like this:

12, 11, 12, 12, 9, 9, 13, 15, 13, 13, 13, 13, 10, 10, 10.

How could this data help you though? To find out the average journey time, or 'mean' as it is also known, you just add the numbers together, then divide the total by how many numbers there are all together. There are 15 numbers in total, adding up to 175, so:

$$175 \div 15 = 11.7$$

That tells you that your mean journey time is 11.7 minutes.

What's in the Middle?

Rather than working out the mean average, you could work out the 'median' instead. This is the data point in the middle of the group. The first thing to do is put the data in ascending order. There are 15 pieces of data, so the median is the 8th number – 12 – shown in bold:

9, 9, 10, 10, 10, 11, 12, **12**, 12, 13, 13, 13, 13, 13, 15.

If there are an even amount of data points, the median is the middle two numbers added together, then divided by 2:

9, 10, 11, 12, 12, **12**, **13**, 13, 13, 13, 13, 15.

In this case, 12 and 13 are the middle numbers, which add up to 25, so the median is $25 \div 2 = 12.5$.

Mostly Modes

A third thing that can be found out is the data point that occurs most often, or 'mode'.

9, 9, 10, 10, 10, 11, 12, 12, 12, **13**, **13**, **13**, **13**, **13**, 15.

In this list, the mode is 13, because it appears five times.

Distorted Data

What would happen if, one day, there was a huge delay and your bus journey took 80 minutes instead of 12? The total of the 15 numbers would be 243 instead of 175, so the mean would increase to 16.2 minutes. This skews your average journey time. This is where the mode and median are useful, as those numbers remain unchanged and can be used as a guide. It goes to show, it's important to try to sort out your data before you come to any conclusions.

GETTING IT SORTED

Imagine that the heights of 1,000 men have been measured and recorded.

A thousand numbers is a lot of data to handle. However, you could sort them into ascending order, then group them into ranges – 140 to 144.9cm, 145 to 149.9cm, and so on. You can then count up the number of people in each range and plot them into a 'histogram', or bar-chart, like this:

height in centimetres

This curved shape is known as 'normal distribution'. In a normal spread of data like this, the mean, median and mode are all in the same place, right in the middle.

By grouping the data like this, you can see that out of the 1,000 men, there were fewer who were at the shorter or taller ends, with more people grouped around the average.

MR VENN'S NUMBER TRAP

Line graphs and bar charts aren't always the most effective way to show data. If you need to show the relationship between different sets of data, a 'Venn diagram' is useful. It was named after John Venn, who came up with the idea in 1880, and consists of overlapping circles, showing different sets of data. The area where the circles overlap represents what the two sets of data have in common.

Give Peas a Chance

If you asked 20 friends if they like ice cream and if they like peas, you could put the results into a Venn diagram according to what they say. In this example, 18 friends have said they like ice cream – only eight like peas as well, and the last two like peas, but not ice cream:

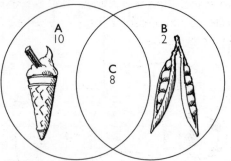

A
10

B
2

C
8

Circle **A** shows the friends who like ice cream. Circle **B** shows the friends who like peas.

Area **C**, where the circles overlap, shows the people who like both ice cream and peas – they are common to both 'sets'.

A Survey of 100 People Says ...

An inventor named Professor X has created a robot – he hopes that it will be extremely popular. Gizmoid can play football and tennis and look after your pet dog while you're at school. It seems like a brilliant idea – football and tennis are very popular, and lots of people have a dog.

To make sure, Professor X does a survey, asking 100 people if they play football or tennis, and if they have a dog. His data shows that 54 people like playing football, 32 play tennis and 46 are dog-owners. Only 3 people don't like football or tennis and don't own a dog.

This sounds very promising, but what's really useful about Venn diagrams is that they can show the relationship between more than two sets of data. If someone doesn't like any of the three things, they are shown outside the circles. So Professor X uses one to see how popular Gizmoid will be.

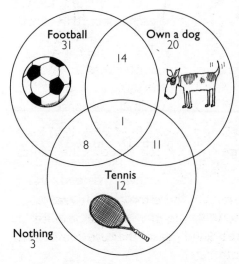

Straightaway, Professor X can see the number of people who share each preference.

So, out of the 100 people Professor X surveyed, only one could make full use of Gizmoid!

A NICE SLICE OF PIE

Remember the creepy-crawly survey on page 65? The survey found 4 earthworms, 16 ants, 3 beetles and 1 slug. Instead of just writing this data as a list though, you could show it visually, using a 'pie chart', with different-sized slices of pie representing the information.

Pie Plotting

You might have a computer that can set out a pie chart for you, in which case, you can tap in your data, sit back and relax. However, if you are drawing a pie chart by hand, your first task is to work out how many degrees each type of creepy-crawly represents.

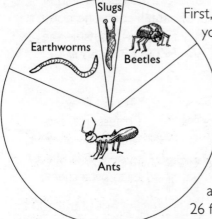

First, you'll need to add up all your creepy-crawlies to get the total – 24. Then you need to work out the fraction of the total that each insect represents.

The 16 ants can be written as $^{16}/_{24}$, which is the same as $^2/_3$, or 0.6̇6̇ as a decimal. (See pages 24 to 26 for a refresher on this.) Multiply 0.6̇6̇ by the 360 ° in a circle and you'll know how much of your pie chart needs to be given to the ants – 240 °. The earthworms need 60 °, the beetles need 45 ° and the slugs need 15 °. Now you can divide your circle up into segments for each one. Note that if you add all these together, the total is 360 °.

WHAT HAPPENS NEXT?

Sometimes it would be very useful to know what could happen in the future. For example, you might want to find out if it's going to rain at the weekend or if it will be sunny when you go on holiday. Even though it's tricky to know for sure, it is possible to say how likely it is that something will happen and express this using numbers.

Oddly Enough

Mathematicians called 'statisticians' – people who are really into statistics – spend their lives working out the 'odds', or chance, of things happening.

For example, the odds of winning the lottery are around 1 in 14 million – so you'd be very lucky to win it. The odds of being struck by lightning are 1 in 3 million – not so lucky, but still very unlikely!

What Are the Chances?

There is a trick to predicting the chance of something happening. You might want to know the likelihood of throwing a dice and getting a six, for instance. To work this out, you would need to count the number of possible outcomes – how many different numbers can be thrown – and what fraction of those a six would be.

There are six possible outcomes when you throw a dice, because it has six sides. However, only one of them is the one you want. This means that the chance of throwing a particular number is one in six.

If you wanted to find out the chance of throwing an even number instead of a particular number, you would need to know how many there are out of the total. There are three even numbers, so the chance of throwing an even number is three in six – the equivalent of one in two. Of course, there is an equal chance of throwing an odd number, too.

How Predictable!

What statisticians are really interested in is 'probability'. This shows, on a scale from zero to one, how likely it is that something will happen:

0	0.5	1
Impossible It definitely won't happen.	**Even Chance** There is as much chance that it will happen as not happen.	**Certain** It definitely will happen.

For example, the probability of a pet goldfish dying at some point is 1, as a goldfish has to die, eventually. You can also express this probability as a fraction or percentage: there is a 100 % probability that a goldfish will die at some point.

To Be Precise

When you are talking about probabilities, it is important to remember that the way you express them can change the meaning. You need to be precise in your description of what is being measured. For example, the probability of a goldfish dying at a particular time, on a particular day, is very different to the probability of a goldfish dying at some point.

A Healthy Hypothesis

Remember Cure-O, the cure for hiccups on page 86? If it was a real medicine, the scientists who were testing it would have to be absolutely sure that it worked safely before it could be used to treat people.

Scientists testing a new medicine formulate what is called a 'hypothesis' – a suggested theory – that they then try to prove or disprove. To do this, they gather and analyse data from tests to work out whether the results are genuine or purely down to chance. They can then decide if the data is statistically significant or not. If the likelihood that the drug is effective is 0.99, or 99%, then they can confidently say that the drug is effective – unlike the imaginary Cure-O, that didn't work at all. Even if the drug works as a cure, there will still need to be tests done to check that it is safe for humans to use!

MASTERFUL MATHS

TOP SECRET!

People have used secret codes to send messages for more than 4,000 years. Some codes are created by swapping letters of the alphabet, or by using symbols, but many rely on mathematics. This science of codes and code-breaking is known as 'cryptography'.

Caesar's Cipher

More than 2,000 years ago, the Roman emperor, Julius Caesar, devised a simple code called a 'transposition cipher'. To make this type of code, you replace each letter in your message with another letter a certain number of places along in the alphabet. Caesar usually went three letters along – so A became D, B became E, and so on.

Frequent Failure

The problem with cipher codes is that they are easy to break. This is because some letters come up more frequently than others and make patterns, which would appear in your cipher, too. For example, in English, the most common letter is E. By looking at a cipher and working out which letter appears most, it is quite easy to see which letter has been substituted for E. If the letter H appears most, you can tell that it is most likely that each letter in the message has been changed for one three letters along in the alphabet.

In 1465, an Italian named Leon Alberti published the first known 'frequency table', which showed how often letters appeared and helped people to decode simple ciphers.

Is It Polybius?

A code that was a little more effective than the simple substitution cipher was created by a Greek man named Polybius, in around 200 BCE. His code involved placing the letters of the alphabet in a grid.

	1	2	3	4	5
1	a	b	c	d	e
2	f	g	h	i/j	k
3	l	m	n	o	p
4	q	r	s	t	u
5	v	w	x	y	z

To encode a message with the Polybius square, you replace each letter with two numbers – the row number, followed by the column number. The letter H, for example, becomes 23. Try using the square to decode the following message (the solution is shown below):

54, 34, 45, 51, 15   13, 42, 11, 13, 25, 15, 14   24, 44, 43, 45, 35, 15, 42, 43, 31, 15, 45, 44, 23!

Unlocking The Square

It's still quite easy to crack this code, once you've worked out that the most frequent letter, 'E', is represented by the number '15'. However, you could add a 'cipher key' – a word that changes the way the alphabet is arranged in your Polybius square

	1	2	3	4	5
1	z	e	b	r	a
2	c	d	f	g	h
3	i/j	k	l	m	n
4	o	p	q	s	t
5	u	v	w	x	y

– to make things trickier. This way, when someone sends you a message and you both have the same key – for example, 'zebra', those letters would be put into the square first, followed by the rest of the alphabet. A code-breaker would have to know the key, too, in order to fit the other letters in the right place and decode your message.

You've cracked it, Supersleuth!

COMPLETING THE ENIGMA

An encryption machine that looked a little like a typewriter, known as the Enigma machine, was invented in the 1920s and was used by Germany during the Second World War. When a message was typed into it, a series of rotors scrambled it into cipher text to keep the communication secret.

The Enigma machine encryption was extremely complex, with so many possible combinations that many people believed it was unbreakable. What's more, the key code was changed daily at midnight. However, a group of people still worked tirelessly to try to crack the code. Alan Turing (see page 114) and his colleagues at Bletchley Park, in England, had an Enigma machine and an electromagnetic machine called a Bombe.

By putting in short parts of a message, known as cribs, that they had already been able to decipher, they were able to use the Bombe to disprove incorrect settings and find the correct ones. It is said that this top-secret project to crack the Enigma code helped to shorten the Second World War.

Computer Encryption

Information can now be encrypted and decrypted by computers in the blink of an eye. The internet, banking details, emails – all encoded in more and more complex ways. Sometimes, these codes are cracked by hackers, who have to use evermore ingenious ways of getting the information.

THE X FACTOR

An area of maths called 'algebra' can be used to calculate quantities when you have some of the information you need already. All you have to do is balance the 'equation' – a calculation where both sides balance.

Easy Equations

An equation, such as '$x = 2 + 1$', might seem a bit odd at first glance, but there is an easy way of thinking of equations that will help you to work them out. Imagine a pair of old-fashioned scales with the equation sitting in them. Everything to the left of the equals sign must balance everything to the right. The solution – the value of x – will have the same value as whatever is on the other side. You know that $2 + 1$ is 3, so if the scales are to balance, x must be 3 as well.

$$3 = 2 + 1.$$

Simple Subtracting

You might also come across equations such as '$x + 1 = 2$'. It looks a little trickier than the one above, but the rule that each side must balance still applies. To find out the value of x this time, you need to rearrange the equation, so that x is on one side of the equals sign, by itself:

'$x + 1 = 2$' is the same as '$x = 2 - 1$'.

In other words, $x = 1$, so the equation is simply $1 + 1 = 2$.

Multiplication Muddles

Sometimes, you might come across an equation where you have to multiply to get the answer:

$$x \times 3 = 10 \times 2 + 1$$

The way the right-hand side of the equation has been written is confusing. Is it $10 \times 2 = 20 + 1 = 21$, or $10 \times 3 = 30$? The way that mathematicians get round this is by using brackets and working out what's inside first. So, with:

$$x \times 3 = 10 \times (2 + 1)$$

it is easy to see that $x \times 3 = 10 \times (3)$, which is 30.

Since $x \times 3 = 30$, to find x, you must divide the answer on the right by the 3 on the left, so if:

$$x \times 3 = 30$$

it's the same as saying $x = 30 \div 3$. x must be 10.

What Is Algebra For?

You may be looking at all these equations wondering what the point is of algebra. It might seem like a lot of bother to work out that $x = 1$ or $x = 10$, but this can come in useful in all sorts of subjects, as well as maths.

For example, in physics, many important laws, such as Galileo's law of fall (see pages 69 to 70), are simplified as equations. They are also used in chemistry, accounting and even geography.

NICE ONE, SHERLOCK

Logic is an area of mathematics that, like so many others, originated in ancient Greece. Logic is used to prove theories and ideas using strict, formal methods and systems.

Logically Speaking

Traditionally, logic was thought of as a branch of philosophy – the study of thought and ideas. One of the most famous examples of logic is a 'syllogism' – a three-statement pattern. This one relates to the Greek thinker, Socrates:

All people are mortal.
Socrates is a person.
Therefore Socrates is mortal.

Logic doesn't tell you whether the statements are true, but it can be used to work out the idea of the statements and what must follow, if they are true. For instance, if it turned out that Socrates wasn't actually a person, but a statue, then the concluding statement would be false. It would be more correct to write the statements like this:

If it is true that
All people are mortal.
And it is also true that
Socrates is a person.
Then it must be true that
Socrates is mortal.

This is now definitely okay, whether Socrates is a person or a statue.

Applying Logic

A logical approach like this can be useful in mathematics.
It makes you look at the structure of what is said and helps
you to pinpoint problems with statements. You can also use
it to make sure that anything you are working out is
expressed correctly.

Logic Reinvented

In the 19th century, a mathematician named George Boole
realized that the way in which logic was used in philosophy
could also be used in algebra. This became known as
'Boolean algebra'.

Boole's work was picked up in the 20th century by three
notable mathematicians – Gottlob Frege, Bertrand Russell
and Alfred Whitehead. They wanted to show that by
employing certain fixed rules, any mathematical theory
could be proved with logic.

A MATHS MACHINE

The first counting device was the abacus, which was in use as early as 4,000 years ago. Over the centuries, many other counting machines were developed – including Charles Babbage's Difference Engine, in 1822. Using a series of toothed wheels, it could make calculations and store data.

Switch On, Switch Off

The development of the kind of computers used these days was thanks to logic, and it started with the flick of a switch.

The flip-flop – not the type you wear on your feet – is a type of switch that can be used to store information. It was invented in the early 20th century.

If a pulse of electricity was sent to the circuit with the flip-flop switch, it triggered a bulb to light up.

A second pulse, and the bulb went out again. It doesn't sound very impressive, does it? However, this allowed the trigger circuit to store information – the fact that a pulse of electricity had been received – in the most simple way possible.

It may not seem much of breakthrough now, and it didn't cause a great deal of excitement at the time either. However, by grouping lots of trigger circuits together, it was possible to store a sequence of pulses as a row of bulbs, some lit, others unlit.

Back To Binary

Here's where the flip-flop switch gets interesting. If you give the 'On' and 'Off' bulbs the numbers '1' and '0', it starts to look more and more like binary code (see pages 12 to 13). Here, the light-bulb sequence is:

| ON | OFF | OFF | ON |

or, 1001 as a binary number. If you remember the columns of 1s, 2s, 4s and 8s, that means one 8 and one 1, or 9:

8s	4s	2s	1s
1	0	0	1

By linking electronic circuits together, the sequences of lights in two rows of bulbs could be added together – in other words, they could be used to do calculations. Different circuits could also be set up to affect each other in different ways. For instance, they could be connected so that if either or both of two bulbs was lit, then a third bulb would be lit.

DO YOU REALIZE WHAT THIS MEANS? WE'VE INVENTED DISCO LIGHTS!

If neither was lit, then the third would be off, too, like this:

Bulb 1	Bulb 2	Bulb 3

This type of circuit is known as a logic circuit. It represents the idea that if one or other thing is true, then a third thing is true, too (see page 102).

Early Days

There is great debate about which computer was the first to be built. However, they were all enormous, filling entire rooms, were very expensive and needed many people to operate them.

A Computer in Your Pocket

In the late 1960s, the development of an 'integrated circuit', known as the 'microchip', enabled much smaller computers to be made. The home computer had arrived. The first ones had limited memories – as little as 16KB – with programmes loaded and stored on cassettes. Just four decades later, people can use their mobile phones with many gigabytes of memory, to browse the internet.

PROVE IT

Every new theorem must be proved before it can be accepted – and there are lots of ways to show proof.

Upside-Down Thinking

To find out if a statement is true, make the opposite statement. If that can be disproved, the first statement must be true. This is called 'proof by contradiction'.

One of the best examples of proof by contradiction was a challenge solved by the Swiss mathematician, Leonhard Euler. The challenge asked if it was possible to cross each of the seven bridges joining the four districts of Königsberg, in Sweden, only once. To try every possible route would be extremely time-consuming, but Euler worked out the answer using proof by contradiction – all without leaving his comfy chair.

The first step was to assume that there definitely was a route where every bridge could be crossed just once. He quickly reasoned that for every bridge to be crossed once, there would have to be an even number of bridges. If there was only one bridge, you couldn't enter and leave a district without crossing it twice – if there were three, you could enter by one and leave by another, but the third would be left uncrossed. As there were seven bridges, Euler had proved by contradiction that there was no possible route where the bridges could all be crossed just once.

ARGUING IN CIRCLES

PLEASE
IGNORE
THIS
NOTICE

This unusual sign is an example of a 'paradox' – something which is absurd, or contradicts itself. It is impossible to do as it says. There are lots of paradoxes around. Some of them are just for fun, but others have been used to test the limits of mathematics.

The Barber Paradox

> 'A barber only shaves the men
> who do not shave themselves.'

This statement is a paradox that was said to have been written by a man named Bertrand Russell. It is absurd because it leads to a contradiction – if the barber were to shave his own beard, it would make him one of the men who shave themselves, so he couldn't be a barber.

The Incomplete Theorem

In 1931, an Austrian mathematician named Kurt Gödel published his 'incompleteness theorem'. It proved that in any complex logical system, there must be some statements that cannot be proved or disproved, and that the system will have gaps that can't be filled. He also showed that mathematics is one of these systems. That means there must be some parts of maths that can't be proved and others that will never be found. If they can't be found, no one even knows what they are – confusing!

MASTERS OF MATHS

You've already heard about some of the work the finest mathematicians in history have done. Now here is a little more about just some of the people who have made mind-blowing discoveries over the centuries.

Pythagoras
(Around 580 BCE to around 500 BCE)

A Greek mathematician who is often credited with coming up with the theorem named after him. Pythagoras and his followers believed that everything could be described with numbers. He also discovered irrational numbers. Little else is known about him and his followers, apart from the fact that they weren't allowed to eat beans or meat! (See pages 20–21 for more on Pythagoras.)

Euclid
(Around 325 BCE to around 265 BCE)

Euclid was a Greek mathematician who wrote a 13-volume guide to geometry called *The Elements*. It is still regarded as a masterpiece of mathematical logic, and this branch of geometry is named 'Euclidean geometry' after him, but little is known of Euclid's life.

Archimedes
(Around 287 BCE to around 212 BCE)

The Greek mathematician, Archimedes, calculated pi with astonishing accuracy for the time. He also measured the area of geometric shapes and was an inventor.

Leonardo Pisano Fibonacci
(1170 to 1250)

This Italian mathematician, who gave his name to the Fibonacci sequence, spent many years travelling. Back at home, he encouraged people to adopt the best methods he had found, such as using the digits 0 to 9, with his most famous work, the *Liber Abaci*, or 'Book of Calculation'.

Galileo Galilei
(1564 to 1642)

Galileo was probably the first scientist to realize that the laws of the Universe are mathematical. He helped prove that the planets go around the Sun, explained the way that objects swing and fall, and used one of the first telescopes to study the night sky. His ideas were so radical that he was put on trial in 1634, and sentenced to house arrest for the rest of his life.

Johannes Kepler
(1571 to 1630)

Kepler managed to work out the mathematical laws that describe the way the planets move round the Sun. He realized that the planets move in elliptical orbits and that their speed is not constant.

René Descartes
(1596 to 1650)

René Descartes not only invented modern graphs and co-ordinates, he was also the first to use letters to represent unknown quantities in calculations.

Pierre de Fermat
(1601 to 1665)

CLEAR OFF, FERMAT – I THOUGHT OF IT FIRST!

Fermat made discoveries in the theory of numbers, geometry and optics and so, unfortunately, did René Descartes. The two spent a great deal of time arguing about who was right and who was first. As Fermat never – for some odd reason – published anything, most of his work is known now through his letters. His 'Last Theorem' is one of the most famous in mathematics and wasn't proved until 1995.

COME OUTSIDE AND SAY THAT, DESCARTES!

Sir Isaac Newton
(1642 to 1717)

Along with Albert Einstein, Sir Isaac Newton is regarded as one of the greatest scientists ever. He came up with mathematical laws to explain the way objects move and the way that gravity affects them. As a result, he was able to work out the motions of the Moon, planets and comets. Many of his theories were published in his greatest work, *Mathematical Principles of Natural Philosophy*.

Gottfried Leibniz
(1646 to 1716)

Leibniz developed several new areas of mathematics, including logic and 'calculus' – a branch of mathematics related to algebra and geometry. He spent years arguing with Sir Isaac Newton about which of them had invented calculus, and even invented one of the first mechanical calculating machines.

Leonhard Euler
(1707 to 1783)

Swiss mathematician, Leonhard Euler, published many papers and books covering every area of mathematics from algebra to trigonometry. Even after he lost his sight in 1766, he continued to produce mathematical papers until he died.

Carl Friedrich Gauss
(1777 to 1855)

YES!

Carl Friedrich's talent for mathematics emerged at a very early age. He made major discoveries in many areas, including statistics, the theory of numbers and geometry – he also correctly calculated the next sighting of the dwarf planet, Ceres.

Albert Einstein
(1879 to 1955)

The German-American physicist, Albert Einstein, often complained that he was no good at maths. In spite of this, he still came up with a new mathematical theory of gravity, which improved on Sir Isaac Newton's. He also showed how time can slow down or speed up, and came up with the most famous equation in the world, $e = mc^2$. Not bad for someone who said he was no good at maths!

Kurt Gödel
(1906 to 1978)

As well as showing that mathematics contains unfillable gaps and unprovable statements, Kurt Gödel also explored the idea of time travel.

Alan Turing
(1912 to 1954)

During the Second World War, the Enigma machine was used by Germany to encrypt messages (see page 99). Drawing on the work of Polish mathematicians, such as Marian Rejewski, Turing and his colleagues finally cracked the code, even though it had been thought to be unbreakable. This work helped to bring the war to an end.

Srinivasa Ramanujan
(1887 to 1920)

Indian mathematician, Srinivasa Ramanujan, showed an incredible talent for mathematics, even as a child. By the time he was in his teens he was coming up with his own theories. Sadly, he died aged just 32, but in that time he had written many papers.

Sir Andrew Wiles
(1953 to present)

A mathematics professor at Princeton, USA, Wiles finally proved Fermat's Last Theorem in 1995. It took ten years to work out and 200 pages to write down.

A NUMBER OF NUMBER TRICKS

If you want to impress friends with your magical abilities and impress your teachers with your startling mathematical skills, these next few pages are for you!

There is a selection of amazing number tricks, mathematical shortcuts and tips, and a collection of mathematical mnemonics, to help with memorizing handy bits of maths.

Trick One: Marvellous Mind-Reading

For this trick, all you need is a friend and a calculator.

1. Ask your friend to think of a three-digit number where the first and last digits are at least two numbers apart. For example, 923 would be fine, because 9 and 3 differ by six – 253 wouldn't work because 2 and 3 are too close.

2. Now ask your friend to reverse their number, so for example, 923 becomes 329.

3. Next ask them to subtract whichever is the smaller number from the larger number, using the calculator if they wish. 923 – 329 = 594.

4. Next, ask them to reverse their answer, so 594 becomes 495. Note that, at this point, the pair of numbers should always be 594 and 495.

5. Finally, ask them to add both answers together – so 594 + 495. Hold up your hand and say, 'Don't tell me, I know the answer!'

6. Pause for effect, then say, 'Is your answer 1,089?' and wait for your friend to gasp in amazement.

Trick Two: Secret Assistant

This trick needs a secret assistant in the audience who is fairly good at mental arithmetic and who can also act surprised on cue. You will also need at least three more people to impress. You'll need to make a few preparations to make sure this trick works well. Here's what to do:

The preparations:

Before your audience is in place, agree on a number with your assistant that is larger than 6,000 to go into the envelope in step 1.

Your assistant will need to be able to subtract the numbers decided on in steps 3, 4 and 5 from the agreed number – this will be where mental arithmetic comes in.

In step 6, they will have this answer ready to use as the year they have 'chosen', and can jot it down with the number you both agreed on written underneath.

The performance:

1. Begin your trick by saying, 'I'm thinking of a number,' in a dramatic voice. With a flourish, write down the number that you agreed with your assistant – 7,684, for example, and seal it in an envelope.

2. Leave the envelope on view for the audience for the rest of the trick – make sure that they can see it clearly.

3. Ask a member of the audience which year they were born in and write their answer on a large sheet of paper – 1973, for example.

4. Now ask another person for a memorable year in their life, 2009 perhaps, and write that down as well.

5. Ask a third person to give you a notable year from history – 1066, for example – and write that down, too.

6. Tell your audience that you will make the trick harder by asking someone to choose another year – past or future – and that they should write it down at the end of your list, but so that you can't see it. Make sure you choose your secret assistant for this job! They will need to write down the number they have worked out during the trick. Using the numbers from steps **3**, **4** and **5** as examples, their year should be 2636 because 1,973 + 2,009 + 1,066 + 2,636 is 7,684.

7. Now ask your assistant to 'add up' all four numbers in your list ready to announce the total. While they are adding up, pass the sealed envelope to another member of the audience.

8. When your assistant announces that the number is 7,684, your audience will be amazed when they open the envelope and discover that the numbers are the same!

TIPS AND SHORTCUTS

When you are working with numbers, there are often useful shortcuts that can help you to find a speedy solution. Here are just a few to get you started.

Dividing by Five

It can be tricky to divide by five, unless you learn all the answers by heart, but dividing by 10 is much easier. Any number that you need to divide by 5 can be divided by 10 and then doubled to find the answer, because $5 = 10 \div 2$.

For example, $90 \div 5$ might seem difficult at first glance, but $90 \div 10$ is much more straightforward – the answer is 9.

Then you can easily double the answer to get 18, so:

$$90 \div 5 = 18$$

Try it for a larger calculations: $280 \div 5$, for example – and it still works. $280 \div 10 = 28$, $28 \times 2 = 56$, so $280 \div 5 = 56$.

Is It Divisible?

Want to guess how a number can be divided? There are some simple tricks to help you work things out.

If a number is divisible by …

… 3, its digits will add up to a multiple of 3. For example, you can tell that 8,904 is divisible by 3 because $8 + 9 + 4$ comes to 21.

… 4, the last two digits will either be two zeros, or will be divisible by 4.

… 10, it will always end in zero.

Elevenses

To multiply a number by 11, first multiply your number, for example 425, by 10, so 425 × 10 = 4,250. Then add the first number to your answer, so 4,250 + 425 = 4,675.

Nine More, Please

When you're multiplying by nine, there's an easy trick to get to the answer quickly.

1. Spread out your hands with your palms facing you.

2. Bend the finger or thumb corresponding to the number you want to multiply 9 by. For 9 × 4, bend the fourth finger on your left hand.

3. Count the thumb and fingers to the left of the bent finger ... 3 in this case. This is the number of 10s in the answer.

4. Now count the fingers and thumb to the right ... 6 in this case. This is the number of ones, so, the answer is 36.

Quick Calculations

Adding up a list of numbers can be daunting, especially if they are not whole numbers. Take this list:

$$73.4 + 98.0 + 61.9 + 83.1 + 3.6 + 56.6 + 64.1 + 50.0 = 490.7$$

If you only want a rough answer, then rounding them all to the closest digit before adding makes less difference than you might think:

$$73 + 98 + 62 + 83 + 4 + 57 + 64 + 50 = 491$$

If you really want to save time, you could round them to the nearest 10 for a rough total, which is still less than 3 % out:

$$70 + 100 + 60 + 80 + 0 + 60 + 60 + 50 = 480$$

How Old Am I?

This cunning trick will let you guess someone's age, using nothing more than the powers of calculation. This trick will work on anyone over the age of ten, so it's perfect for amazing your teachers or your parents. Here's how to do it:

1. Ask your chosen person to multiply the first number of his or her age by five, but to keep this number secret from you. For example, if your chosen person is 23, they would multiply 2×5, to get 10.

2. Ask your chosen person to add three to the number he or she has just calculated. The 23-year-old person would add 3 to 10, to get 13. All the calculations should be being done secretly, so you don't hear what numbers the person is using.

3. Ask your chosen person to double the number he or she has just worked out. So, for example, your 23-year-old would multiply 13 x 2 to get 26.

4. Next up, your chosen person should add the second digit of his or her age to the figure they got in step **3**. Your example person – maybe his name is Joe – would add three to 26, giving him 29. Ask your chosen person to tell you this number.

5. Now, all you have to do is subtract six from the number that your chosen person has told you, and voilà, this new number will be his or her age.

This trick should work no matter how old the person is – just like magic!

MATHEMATICAL MNEMONICS

A 'mnemonic' is something that can help you remember things. Sometimes it is a rhyme, or it can be an 'acronym' — a word made up of the first letter of each word in a list. PIN, for example, is an acronym for Personal Identification Number.

MY NEW ELEPHANT MUNCHES ONLY NEW IMPORTANT CARS.

How Many Days?

Whether you're counting down the days until your birthday, or trying to work out the day you were born on, this rhyme comes in handy:

> 30 days hath September,
> April, June and November
> And all the rest have 31
> Except for February alone
> Which has 28 days clear
> And 29 in each leap year.

How I Wish I Could Remember Pi!

Remembering pi to more than a couple of decimal places might be less difficult than it seems at first. All you need is a rhyme or sentence where each word has the corresponding number of letters to the numbers in pi. For example, 'How I wish I could calculate pi before lunch, for lunch includes fantastic rounded dumplings,' gives you pi to 14 places:

$$3.14159265358979$$

A Fraction Reminder

In a fraction (see pages 24 to 26), which number is the numerator, and which is the denominator? Use this as a reminder:

NUmerator Up,
Denominator Down

Mean, Mode Or Median?

When you're dealing with data and averages (see pages 87 to 88), how do you remember what mean, mode and median each mean? It's quite muddling.

Mode and **mo**st both have four letters and both start with '**mo**'. You can remind yourself with a sentence like this:

'There once was a mean average. He had a median caught in the middle. The mode appeared most.'

Compass Directions

To make good use of the maps on pages 77 to 81, you'll need to know which way north, south, east and west are. Use one of these mnemonics to remember them clockwise from the top, where north is:

'Never Eat Shredded Wheat,' or,
'Never Eat Slimy Worms.'

INDEX

125